Making Life More Livable

**Simple adaptations for the homes
of blind and visually impaired older people.**

by
IRVING R. DICKMAN

American Foundation for the Blind
New York

Irving R. Dickman is author of numerous publications in the area of blindness and visual impairment. AFB published his *Outreach to the Aging Blind* in 1977. Among the pamphlets he has written for the Public Affairs Committee are: *Living with Blindness; What Can We Do About Limited Vision?* and *A Vision Impairment of the Later Years: Macular Degeneration*

Project Editor
C. Michael Mellor
Consultants
Mary Ellen Mulholland
Debra Budick
Robert E. O'Donnell
Lorraine G. Hiatt

Phyllis Levy
Vernon Metcalf
Eugene F. Murphy
Joan Ord
Leon A. Pastalan
Carolyn Schumacher
Anne Yeadon

Library of Congress Cataloging in Publication Data
Dickman, Irving R.
    Making life more livable.

    Bibliography: p.
    1. Aged, Visually handicapped. 2. Self-help devices for the disabled—Handbooks, manuals, etc.
1. Title
HV1597.5.D498   1983   640'.2408161   83-6412
ISBN 0-89128-115-0

Cover Photos: Janet Charles

Published by American Foundation for the Blind
11 Penn Plaza, Suite 300, New York, NY 10001
Printed in the United States of America

Contents

Introduction

Contrary to popular stereotypes, not all older people are worn out, impoverished, feeble, useless wrecks. Many are still active and have an impressive range of skills and coping mechanisms to make their later years enjoyable and productive.

Still, the passage of time leaves its mark, and one problem that affects many older people is progressive deterioration of their eyesight. But poor vision in old age does not have to be a catastrophe. Changes in the home, often relatively minor, along with some order and organization can enable the person with poor vision to live as he or she has been used to living. This handbook does not set out to solve all the problems faced by an older person with deteriorating vision; it describes some solutions that *have* worked for some people and demonstrates that with a little common sense, ingenuity, and a bit of thought, vision loss does not necessitate a complete change in an individual's way of life.

In the United States today, some 75-80 percent of all men and women over 65 live in their own homes and apartments. But for the two-thirds of these older people whose vision has become noticeably weaker, the comforts of home may dwindle: television becomes radio, sewing and hobbies become guessing games, and the joys of cooking become fond memories. Worse, for those with the most severe vision problems, home may no longer be the safe haven it used to be. Steps become icy slides, a hallway is a perilous passage, a coffee table a booby-trap; and even a half-inch high threshold can become a dangerous obstacle if attention flags.

The difficulties of older people are made worse if family and friends regard the impaired vision as a sign of failing memory, or even of reduced intelligence. In some cases older people who could not see well enough to manage entirely on their own have been mistakenly placed in nursing homes and other institutions.

There are usually better options. It is true that vision itself may not be fully restored, though drugs can control glaucoma, and cataract surgery is usually very effective. There are, however, ways of making more effective use of whatever vision remains. And in recent years architects, designers, engineers, environmental psychologists, social workers, agencies for blind and visually impaired people— and older people themselves — have begun to focus on ways of improving the quality of home life. They have concluded that much can be done to adapt the home, the tools, and the tasks of daily living (and visually impaired people themselves,

through training) to make life safer, easier, and more enjoyable.

No General Prescriptions

This handbook is designed to fill a gap, to look at certain problems and problem areas in the home, and to explore some approaches to dealing with them effectively. At the outset, it must be made clear that there can be no general prescriptions. No two people have the same type and degree of visual loss, the same kind of lifestyle, the same kind of home, the same needs and wants and likes. Furthermore, there are usually several ways, or combinations of ways, to deal with a problem. Solutions must be individual, tailor made. And given the realities of today's economy, they should be simple, practical, and inexpensive. If the older person can make the adaptation himself or herself, that is ideal. But at least it should be possible for a relative, friend, or handy neighbor to carry out the adaptation. It should not be necessary to be or wait for an expert.

The suggestions in this handbook are no more than a sampling; with a little encouragement anyone can come up with other, perhaps better, adaptations. It is for this reason that we have also indicated the underlying principles for such adaptations—the fruit of research already done. Approaches which turn out to be beneficial to older people with impaired vision will also prove helpful to all older people. Indeed, safer and more convenient kitchens and stairways, better lighted work and study areas, safer and more functional appliances are a boon to all people of all ages.

Adaptations: Some General Comments

Simple adaptations to the home, in combination with adaptive or sensory training, can help an older person achieve better visual functioning and improve and enrich the quality of the home environment. Dr. Leon A. Pastalan, co-director of the National Policy Center on Housing and Living Arrangements for Older Americans (University of Michigan), suggests that feeling "independent" is the most important aspect of an older person's quality of life.

Modifications and adaptations for older visually impaired people are an excellent investment for society as well. Not only because one day everyone grows old (and many will have impaired vision), but also because planning and constructing the physical environment to make it more suitable for persons with impaired vision makes daily life easier for everybody.

What Is Poor Vision?

Visual acuity is usually expressed as a Snellen score — the familiar 20/20 fraction, which means perfect vision. What this score says is that at 20 feet a person can read a precisely defined line on the eye chart. With 20/200 vision, a person can see at 20 feet what someone with perfect vision would be able to see at 200 feet. A score of less than 20/200 with best correction is one definition of "legal blindness." The other definition concerns the visual field — essentially how far to the side a person can see when looking straight ahead. An individual is said to be legally blind if the area he or she can see, with the best possible correction, is no more than 20 degrees in the eye with the largest field. (For comparison, the normal visual field covers some 180 degrees.) Legal blindness entitles a person to certain tax and social security benefits.

A person who is legally blind does not live in a world of total darkness. Indeed 80 percent or more of people loosely called blind can see. At the very least such a man or woman may be able to detect the presence or absence of light (this is called light perception). Some people are able to tell from which direction light is coming (light projection), and others can see the outlines of objects. With certain eye conditions it may be possible to read, but not to walk around easily because side vision has deteriorated (tunnel vision). On the other hand, a person may be able to walk around easily but be unable to read because central vision has been lost. In some eye conditions, the individual has blind spots, and the vision of some people fluctuates from day to day and at different times of the day. (See p. 6-7 for examples of what people can typically see with various eye conditions.)

Each type of vision impairment obviously creates a different kind of seeing problem. Useful as acuity scores are for some purposes, they are little help in determining the needs of a specific individual. Fifty elderly persons may have identical visual acuity scores, but they will almost certainly have fifty different sets of problems to cope with at home. There are too many variables: not only the amount and type of visual loss, but also others, having to do with what the home is like and what characterizes each individual's lifestyle: even with 20/20 vision, not everyone wants to cook, play chess, or whittle.

Depending on the person and the home, modifications to compensate for poor vision may need only an adjustment or two — place a chair in a different position, paint a wall white, put a different bulb in the bedside lamp. In another case there may be many suggestions, each designed to suit that person with that lifestyle in that place. (Each problem is individual; each solution will have to be individual too.)

The key: *how* the individual functions. How *well* he or she functions. How well he or she *wants* to function.

PHOTO: JANET CHARLES

Few visually impaired older people lose all their vision. These photographs suggest what people can still see despite eye conditions associated with aging. 1. Cataract: There is annoying glare around the lights and general loss of detail elsewhere. 2. Glaucoma: If not treated soon enough, glaucoma can destroy peripheral ("side") vision, leaving "tunnel vision" — a small area in which a person can still see. 3. Macular degeneration: Central vision is lost, making it difficult to read or do close work, but objects can still be detected with side vision. 4. Diabetic retinopathy: This condition can leave blind spots, but some vision remains intact.

PHOTO: JANET CHARLES

3

4

Involve the Older Person

In any home, many adaptations will already have been made and small improvements added over time. But people may never get around to other changes. All it may take is a question, a suggestion, a helping hand to start. In still other cases, it is possible that much more may be needed to make life livable again. When changes have *not* been made as a result of helplessness, or apathy, or both, it becomes even more critical to consult and involve the elderly man or woman.

It is best for older persons themselves to think about and make adaptations. If that isn't possible, here's some advice from practitioners: "Go and look first," says Phyllis Levy, supervisor of community rehabilitation teaching, New York Association for the Blind (the Lighthouse). "Second, see what *you* think is needed. Third, ask the client what *he* or *she* thinks is needed. Fourth, *always* follow the client's decision."

Respect for the older friend or relative means allowing him or her to reject suggestions — even for what seem to be the wrong reasons: A change might be rejected not on how it works, but because of how it looks. The individual may feel embarrassed by too visible adaptations.

For example, in a U.S. Department of Housing and Urban Development

(H.U.D.) survey, where the problem was of giving better access to kitchen cabinets, most older people favored such ideas as pull-out drawers and sliding doors, but more than three-quarters thought taking the doors off cabinets altogether was a bad idea. Those people known to be visually impaired were even more opposed—over 83 percent against.

Involve the older person. Don't take helplessness for granted. "Many of the things we do," says Vernon Metcalf, executive director of the Florida Association of Workers for the Blind (Miami Lighthouse), "were thought up by somebody else, by one of the clients, or one of their family or friends: 'Why don't you do this?' and it turns out to be something we never thought of. So we try it, and surprisingly often it works fine."

Hazards and Obstacles

In taking that first look at the home, it is important to remember that many elements that are not especially hazardous to younger people may be a problem to older people with visual impairments, particularly if other disabling conditions such as arthritis are present. Older people may in any case have slow reaction times and reduced ability to recover from stumbles. Any previous accidents will of course provide clues. A walk-through, a few hours' conversation (with the visually impaired woman or man), will highlight other problems, or potential problems.

Here are some possible hazards:

Doors: Many older people tend to look at the floor as they walk — to avoid tripping and falling — and sometimes run into doors (including cabinet doors) that have been left ajar. Depending on other disabling conditions, and practical remodeling considerations, it might be best to convert problem doors to sliding doors. Even consider removing them altogether — a major purpose of room doors is to provide privacy, but that may not be important for a person living alone.

If privacy is needed for guests, curtains might well do the trick. Curtains also make it easier for wheelchair users to pass through doorways.

If the older person does not want to remove doors, then he or she should remember to either open doors *all* the way or close doors *all* the way. Visitors should be reminded to observe this rule too.

Floor coverings: A major cause of accidents, floor coverings should always be checked. Rug corners and edges should be tacked and/or taped down. Small area rugs may be removed if they prove dangerous, but remember that they can be useful in defining areas for a person with poor vision. Worn and torn carpeting and linoleum should be taken up and replaced. Cover bare and potentially slippery floors with textured runners or carpeting. Don't

A very small adaptation can make a big difference. Simply draping a towel over the back of a
chair makes it far easier to see and reduces the
likelihood that you will accidentally bump into it.

wax linoleum. Plain, unpatterned linoleum may be less confusing than patterned linoleum.

Thresholds/doorsills: It is almost impossible to believe that objects less than an inch high can do so much damage. But doorsills are a major cause of falls — especially for people wearing badly or loosely fitting slippers or shoes. This danger is so great that the American National Standards Institute (ANSI) suggests that thresholds be flush, beveled, or planed down to no more than ¼ inch high, and be brightly colored.

Furniture: Despite the understandable reluctance an older person might show, some rearrangement of furniture should be considered — with permission of the older person, of course. Sharp edges can be lethal; low coffee tables almost guarantee barked shins or worse. Where it is not possible to move such items out of main circulation areas, some sort of bright padded cover, a towel, or tablecloth, especially at edges and corners, could be used to make these potential obstacles more conspicuous.

Optical aids: While this handbook focuses on adapting the home to the individual—a relatively new approach—this should be done in conjunction with the more traditional means of providing help: adaptive devices, and adapting (training) the individual.

Most older visually impaired people already have an optical aid: prescription spectacles. But when they reach the can't-read-with-them/can't-read- without-them stage they find themselves pretty much cut off from written information, some of it quite essential — food and medicine labels, Social Security and Medicare/Medicaid notices, personal letters, and bills. The trouble is that package, can, and bottle labels are almost always designed by younger eyes: Your 30-year old package designer is not your 80-year old consumer. Label information is almost always too small, or has dark letters on a white/light background with insufficient contrast.

Depending on the type and seriousness of the visual impairment, one of the many kinds of low vision aids might well prove invaluable. Simple hand- and stand-magnifiers, battery lighted magnifiers, even (for the more affluent) a closed circuit TV (CCTV), are available from several sources. Also available are a vast variety of inexpensive task- and activity-oriented aids, including needle threaders, large and/or raised number templates for dial and push-button phones, large size, large print playing cards, adapted chess, checkers, and other games.

Still, the first effort is to make do with what is on hand, even if it might not ordinarily be considered an adaptive aid — a rubber band to identify the bottle of

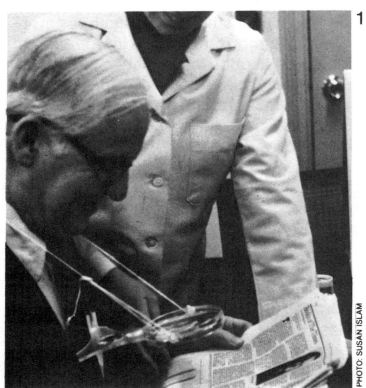

PHOTO: SUSAN ISLAM

PHOTO: JANET CHARLES

Some optical low vision aids: 1. Chest-held magnifier has the advantage of leaving both hands free. 2. Hand-held magnifier. 3. Stand magnifier is especially useful if your hand is not too steady. 4. Telemicroscope allows you to see material without having to get so close to it that you have no room to write.

3

4

13

heart medicine, for example. "Our basic philosophical position," says Vernon Metcalf (Miami Lighthouse), "is to try not to develop or buy any special items, aids or devices for blind and visually impaired people. Instead see what's in the house; if you have to get something, try to use generic equipment that's available for everybody (an off-the-shelf item from the supermarket or hardware store, for instance). Our experience is that the cheapest solution is usually the best. I've always believed that if you can modify something that's already around the house, without going out and buying something special, you're better off... The more complicated the solution, the less likely that it will be used. Sometimes younger people are so anxious to be helpful that we dream up all kinds of things to help people with impaired vision; but we haven't looked: we don't know what's really needed. It looks good on paper, but when the client starts to use it, it doesn't work."

Adapting the Individual

Most adaptive aids take time to adapt *to*. Even a simple magnifying glass takes time to get used to, since it distorts the appearance of the print and has to be held *steady* at the correct distance. A more complicated device is correspondingly more difficult to adjust to, though in the end it may offer great benefits. Sometimes the frustrations are too much: think of the thousands of eyeglasses and hearing aids lying unused in dresser drawers. When that happens, it is often because the professional who dispensed the aid never took the time to train the user in its proper use.

Improving the quality of life in the home may nevertheless require more than training in the use of low vision aids: it may require a retraining in the use of the eyes. Some of the needed services and training are provided by local agencies for blind and visually impaired persons or the Cooperative Extension Service of the U.S. Department of Agriculture. This training is not only in using residual vision, but also in using the other senses as substitutes or supplements, learning to be alert to, and to recognize, environmental cues that are not visual. Part of this sensory training involves encouraging people to use their visual memory, to remember what they saw (and how it looked) when they could see better.

Specific skills are also taught, e.g., cooking, sewing, hobbies, and orientation and mobility (how to get about safely).

Opening the Curtain

Another part of the training is to restore to older people some of their lost confidence; their lost ability to cope, to help themselves. Naturally, friends and relatives can play an important part in this process.

It may be something so simple—like the elderly woman who complained that she was having trouble moving around the house, even during the daylight hours, because there was not enough light. The agency instructor came in, took one look, and persuaded the woman to draw back the heavy curtains she'd had on her windows since she was married.

Other adaptations may be almost as simple: putting in a stronger bulb, moving a lamp closer, moving a table out of the way. Wherever possible, improvement must be economically feasible and uncomplicated.

But more important is another function that friends, relatives, and agency personnel can perform: encouraging the older person to help himself or herself. There's ample evidence that people can regain lost ground. In rental housing, the Department of Housing and Urban Development report indicated, "People [with disabilities] readily develop adaptations of their own, usually by building convenience equipment or using something in a different way than it was intended." The incentive is there: Living with the problems 24 hours a day, older visually impaired people have every incentive to try to help themselves and make life more livable.

Some Basic Concerns

For people with more severe visual impairments, the home that has been a friend and sheltering environment for many years now appears less friendly, even inhospitable — all sharp edges and booby-traps. Getting through the day can be fatiguing and deeply worrisome, because of the far greater amount of energy needed to assimilate visual information. (Imagine the difficulties of moving through a familiar environment wearing someone else's glasses or with rain drops on your own glasses.) But boredom is what elderly visually impaired people most often complain about; lack of recreation is called the greatest loss. Life space — outside the home and even inside it — becomes more and more circumscribed, activities like reading and sewing are dropped, the telephone (and listening to radio or television) become almost the only recreational outlets.

"In general," says Dr. T.R. Cullinan, senior lecturer, Department of Environmental and Preventive Medicine, St. Bartholomew's Medical College, London, "the worse the sight the more likely it is to present the greatest hardship [though] nearly half of the visually disabled are so overwhelmed by other disabilities (chief among them are arthritis and heart disease) that their sight problems recede in significance..." But he adds "among the visually disabled...at least a third of them ascribe *all* their difficulties in mobility and social enjoyment to their poor vision."

Until recently that state of affairs has been accepted as "the way things are," "part of growing old." But now research has begun to raise questions: Is that the way it *has* to be? Dr. Pastalan, speaking not only about the home environment but also about the world outside the door, says that while it is apparently impossible to forestall age-related sensory losses, appropriately adapted environments function as a more effective support network and mitigate the consequences of the aging individual's sensory losses.

The snag is that all too few homes provide that more effective support, and many elderly visually disabled people are living in home conditions that actually exaggerate their disability. In fact, Dr. Cullinan adds, "two-thirds of visually disabled people seemed to see marginally or markedly worse at home that they did under hospital conditions." The chief reason? "Poor home lighting may well be responsible for much of the difference, which tends to affect more those with residual vision than those who can perceive hardly more than light."

Lighting: In fact, Dr. Cullinan points out that general levels of lighting are often so poor in the homes of elderly people that twice as many people as need to function as "blind." Most older people live in environments where light levels are as great an obstacle to vision as site levels are barriers to the wheelchair user.

Lighting may well be the most important factor in adapting the home — and not just for older people. In a 1974 study of 900 young (not disabled) office workers asked to rate the importance to their jobs of twelve environmental factors, good lighting ranked first.

Furthermore, lighting changes are among the least expensive adaptations that can be made in the home environment. Most homes will need only a stronger bulb (though take care not to exceed a lamp's recommended wattage as this could produce excessive heat and even cause a fire), a better placed lamp or ceiling light, and advice about lampshades, curtains, and the placing of chairs. Major and expensive changes, such as rewiring, renewing sockets, or interior decoration, will rarely be necessary.

Paradoxically, it may not always be a matter of *more* light: it may take less. Some people with low vision, particularly those with cataracts, are sensitive to light, sometimes without being aware of it, except that their eyes feel tired and irritated in brightly lit areas.

But even for those who need more light, the solution may *not* involve simply substituting a 200-watt bulb for a less powerful one. Other things must be considered. For example, is the lighting level consistent throughout the house? The effect of shadows, or of going from a brightly lighted area to a dimmer one, or vice versa, is a major cause of missteps and falls. In a home with younger and older people, subdued lighting that is esthetically pleasing to the younger resident may mean impenetrable shadows to the elderly. A "dramatic" bright spot may equate with "slippery," and the dark beyond may look like steps. Yet certain jobs require super-illumination, far beyond what younger eyes need.

Ceiling lighting can be very inconvenient. A good shaded light that illuminates a specific area is usually preferable.

Steps and Stairways: Few homes provide for special lighting in what should definitely be the best lighted areas of the home — steps and stairways. For it is there that falls and other accidents are most likely to occur. Lighting in these areas must be carefully positioned to prevent either glare or shadows, which would simply add to distorted perceptions.

Dimmer switches: When and if the level of

lighting in ceiling and wall fixtures is increased, it is a good idea to replace all wall switches with dimmer switches that can help to prevent sudden lighting level changes at various times of day, and from one room to another. Dimmer switches also provide more flexibility for those days or situations when less rather than more light is needed.

Something similar can be accomplished with lamps. With appropriate switches, three-way bulbs can help to provide whatever lighting intensity is needed in a smaller area, and easily installed dimmer switches for lamps are now on the market.

To experiment with how much lighting is needed, Gilliatt and Baker, in *Lighting Your Home,* suggest clamping a work lamp near a work area and swivelling it around to determine the best direction from which the light should come.

Fluorescents versus Incandescents: For high ambient illumination levels, most experts agree that fluorescent lights are better than incandescents. The reason is obvious: Fluorescents give more brightness for less electricity, making them less expensive to run, though installation costs may be higher. (There are now inexpensive adapters on the market which allow circular fluorescents to be inserted in ordinary lamp sockets.) Many agencies

for the blind and visually impaired, including New York's Center for Independent Living, which deals with older persons, recommend fluorescents, especially for ceiling fixtures.

Still, the harsher, bluish light of fluorescents can be unpleasant — a problem that is reduced in the full spectrum lamps that closely duplicate natural daylight. There are also fluorescents that give out a light similar to that of incandescents.

Another difficulty with fluorescents is that they flicker. This is not usually noticeable, but changes in the structure of the eye's lens make some elderly people sensitive to flicker, which may give them headaches, cause eyes to tear, and lead to general inattentiveness. The buzzing sound fluorescents make can also be distracting (though proper maintenance should reduce buzzing).

Older people, and visually impaired people generally, can see close work better under incandescents rather than fluorescents. The key is contrast. Fluorescent lighting scatters light, and gives far better area lighting than do incandescents. But for reading, or being able to differentiate print from background, the light quality and directionality of incandescents, the fact that the light source in continuous and very stable, make it preferable.

Incandescents should be used for close work — preparing meals, sewing, reading, jigsaw puzzles, a home workshop, playing the piano, or whatever tasks or hobbies are a part of the older person's lifestyle.

Such task-oriented lighting almost always demands more light, but not always the same amount. Sewing by hand, which usually means small needles and small stitches, needs twice as much light as does casual reading.

Glare: Philip C. Hughes (director of Environmental Photobiology, Duro-Test Corporation), and Robert M. Neer (Harvard Medical School), caution that it is not enough that the quantity of light be task-oriented: the quality of the light should also be task related, with specific reference to the level of glare, a major problem for elderly people, because the pupil of the eye contracts too slowly to properly reduce the amount of light entering the eye when the gaze moves to a relatively bright area from one that is less bright. Too much light, especially from a badly positioned source, can therefore actually reduce visibility.

A single light source of 200 watts is much more likely to produce glare than five 40 watt bulbs, separately positioned, though the intensity of lighting may not be quite the same. Direct glare from overhead lighting, especially from bare lamps, can be particularly difficult. Putting a shade on the lamps, or if possible rearranging the work area, can be a great help. Repositioning standing lamps, especially to reduce glare reflected from polished metal surfaces, shiny fixtures, table tops and floor, can be effective. Where possible, this type of glare can also be eliminated through the use of non-reflective materials or polishes. Chrome, and waxed, polished surfaces should be avoided.

Positioning lamps may pose a problem if they need to be moved frequently. Electrical outlets are almost always installed so close to the floor that old people find them hard to reach. If lamps do not need to be used too often, no need for changes. But if an inconveniently placed outlet must be used often, a solution that avoids an expensive rewiring job is to tape or tack an extension outlet to the wall at a more convenient height.

Windows: Artificial lighting is not the only source of glare: For older people with visual impairments, sunlight or simply bright outdoor light streaming through windows into a dark room can be just as troubling. Go into the light airy lounge of a nursing home on a sunny day and you will often find it unoccupied — because what is light, sunny, and cheerful to the younger eyes of architects, designers and staff, is painful and disturbing glare to the eyes of the elderly residents.

For tomorrow's housing there is polarized window glass that reduces glare from outside with little loss of light or change of tint, and prismatic window glass, which diffuses outside light, eliminates shadows, and makes lighting more even throughout. Such elaboration may not be practicable. Nor is it necessary: Existing curtains and drapes can be used to control the amount of glare from outdoor light. Inexpensive adaptations include venetian or vertical blinds, or mylar shades that tint the incoming light. One other suggestion if economics permit: keep ceiling or area lights on even during the day, to equalize lighting from indoor and outdoor sources and reduce the irritating effects of glare on the eye.

Throughout the house, many surfaces reflect the glare of outdoor and artificial light sources. Research indicates that for older people, the most dangerous areas for reflected glare is the floor. Many older people tend to look down as they walk; for some, this stems from a not unrealistic fear of tripping and falling. As a result, that reasonably bright but usually unnoticed (by younger people) floor or kitchen linoleum may look like a car's headlights or a skating rink to older eyes. Until technology provides a wax that will clean linoleum without producing glare, the solution is to forsake brightness and settle for non-shiny, but clean, floors. Wherever a careful walkover shows glare spots on a floor, some sort of matte sur-

Glare from a polished floor near a window disappears when covered by an area rug. Make sure, though, that the rug cannot slip when you walk on it.

face, carpeting, runners or non-slip plastic or rubber matting, may be the answer.

In hallways, shiny floors can provide a little more light, but it might be wiser to keep the bright areas to a strip along the walls, with a darker runner down the center. In fact, painting the walls a light bright color will do even more than shiny floors to lighten a dark hallway.

Colors and Contrasts: The effectiveness of augmented lighting can be enhanced by the use of color. Lighter walls tend to give more light. But if glare from the walls is a problem, dark walls or patterned wallpaper tend to absorb light. For better seeing, in other words, color works both ways. Where painting is possible, and more illumination is important, lighting and a new color scheme should be considered together.

Increasing the lighting level helps to compensate for the normal falloff in the older eye's perception of color. Important as this may be for esthetic reasons, from the point of view of environmental adaptations it is more important that lighting heighten the contrast between two objects, or an object and an area, of a similar color or tone. For example, a white dish and a white napkin on a white tablecloth look like a single undifferentiated blur to the older diner.

Even strong lighting may not help the person with impaired vision to distinguish one color from another in such an instance. Here is a vivid description of what visual impairment can do to color perception. (The comments are by Jessica Finch, writing in the newsletter of the British Retinitis Pigmentosa Society. Bear in mind that the writer's eye condition [retinitis pigmentosa] is not connected with aging):

"The following thoughts and queries were prompted by a face-lift. given to my kitchen a few years ago. Why should having the dark brown chairs painted white make such a difference to the ease with which I moved around the room? The answer, I realized, was that the old brown chairs had been more or less the same tone as the kitchen floor and I was constantly knocking into them. Now the magnolia white paint was a splendid contrast to the dark red and I no longer had any trouble.

"This discovery led me to think further on the subject of contrasting tones. I realized that I had previously left light-colored tea towels on the back of these brown chairs merely to create a contrast. I then wondered why I had not painted the table legs white as well, and found that it had not been necessary because the white table top gave sufficient contrast and it had been better to keep the table legs brown, thus reducing visual confusion. I also asked myself what had prompted me to cover the seats of those chairs with what were, to me, mud colored cushions? (They were in fact a cheerful red

Keep color contrast in mind when you set the table. White plates almost disappear on a white table, but show up well against a plain dark table cloth.

and white check.) The muddy color, for me, had . . . masked the dazzling whiteness of the surface of the chair seat; without breaking up the general shape of the chair it had made looking at it a more restful process. I realized why I liked the dark red floor so much, because I found it provided a restful and undistracting surface on which to look down. This insight also gave me the answer to why the dark red draining board seemed so satisfactory. The darkness absorbed the light coming through the window, and I could concentrate my attention on the things that were on the draining board, such as light colored dishes. The dark draining board, well-cleaned, was an ideal pastry board, because the white flour showed up well against it.

"All these 'discoveries' brought home to me that dark and light tones could help me to see more easily."

Retinitis pigmentosa poses its own special vision problems, but the difficulty in distinguishing colors described above resembles a problem with the aging eye, in which the gradual yellowing of the crystalline lens makes it more difficult to differentiate among colors of a similar intensity, brightness or "greyness."

For younger persons to get some idea of what colors look like to an elderly person, they need only put on a pair of yellow or yellowish-brown sunglasses and wear them for a time indoors. They will find it difficult — if not impossible — to distinguish between pastel blues, lavenders, yellows and pinks; and darker shades of brown and blue and even grey will be hard to tell apart.

Dr. Leon Pastalan's empathic model study (see page 84) found that cool colors — green and blue — tended to fade the most, and red the least. The study found that boundaries tended to disintegrate: closely related colors seemed to blend into each other, while intense contrasting colors seemed to overlap.

If the older person keeps bumping into objects or has difficulty in seeing objects on tables or work areas (like a white dish on a light table cloth), such objects should be thought of in terms of a figure-ground relationship. The greater the contrast, in color and in tone/intensity, the easier it is to see and distinguish objects.

In some cases, the remedy may be to place light objects on dark surfaces, or vice versa. A darker tablecloth, a lighter linoleum on the kitchen floor or in the hallway may make a vast difference. Solid colors are of course better by far — especially on floors — than patterns, stripes or checks, which blend and confuse, and create strange optical illusions, when at a distance from the eyes.

It is better to position a light object against a dark area, rather than vice versa, because the object is more easily seen.

Small things, like a lighter colored switchplate on the wall, or making sure the door knob contrasts in tone and/color with the door can prove very helpful.

If the older person seems to see better at home than in the ophthalmologist's office, it may be because he or she is dealing with familiar places and objects, or *remembering* colors rather than seeing them. So if new painting is a possibility, color preferences should be checked by observation — how they appear now rather than as they are remembered.

Touching and Textures: By far the greatest amount of information about the environment reaches us through the eyes. Therefore, as vision becomes more and more impaired, the amount of useful information concerning the home and other environments gradually decreases. Nevertheless, as the amount of visual information dwindles, it is possible to learn to supplement and reinforce this information with cues from the other senses — touch, hearing, even smell — even if these sensory processes are also not what they used to be.

In fact, these many non-visual cues are always there: unlike seeing, which usually requires a conscious act, sounds and smells are so much there that they have been allowed to fade into the background. Without thinking about it, you know you're approaching the kitchen when you smell the roast cooking in the stove, or hear the hum of the refrigerator.

To make the sense of touch an asset to those with impaired vision, older persons may be helped by some training to make them more aware of the cues that already exist. They can be shown the position of knobs and dials, for example, to tell them when the device is on or off, or what the oven temperature reading is, or where the wash cycle stands. These positions may now have to be learned, because until vision deteriorated there had never been any point to knowing such things.

Or newer kinds of tactile cues can be learned: feeling for the fruit-shaped piece of felt, or the two rubber bands, to determine what is in the can whose label you can't read; learning to distinguish between two dark dresses, one for summer and the other for winter, by the feel of the material; feeling the smooth edge of a nickel and the rough edge of a quarter; feeling for the aperture of a spray can so you direct the spray where you want it.

Touch can also be important in maintaining the ability to move safely in the environment. In a hallway where the lighting is not adequate, touching the walls here and there will provide orientation and balance. Tactile cues can in fact be deliberately added to the environment: strategically placed furniture can help in crossing the seemingly vast spaces of an open living room.

And it is not by hands alone that tactile information is received. In terms of safety, perhaps the most important tactile cues can come through the feet, as when learning to feel for the edges when going down a flight of steps.

Sounds: For many an older man or woman, background noises can be a scourge, because he or she finds them impossible either to understand or ignore. Yet learning to be aware of relevant sounds can provide highly useful environmental clues. That means tuning in what you've always tuned out, listening to what you can't really help hearing — for the useful information sounds provide. It means hearing when you've turned the water off; listening for street noises, if you can't remember whether you shut the window; remembering that the creaking floorboard means that you're coming to the top of the steps; detecting the click which means the washing machine dial is on "dry."

Any number of audible cues can be added to the environment, if and where they're needed: An audible timer, to remind you to turn off the roast, or to tell you when the pie crust should be brown; wind chimes to warn you where the steps are; even a system of bells or a buzzer to let you know when you've left the front door or a closet door ajar — a door you are likely to run into. Such a system can be activated by a switch like that of an automatic closet light.

Room by Room

Given the many differences in individual situations, what follows is at best a sampling of problems and suggestions for dealing with them. These suggestions have another—perhaps more important—purpose: To help older men and women with impaired vision, and their families and friends, not only to focus on specific problems, but also to encourage them to experiment, to work out their own adaptations and find their own solutions.

In the kitchen

Preparing a meal.

Attach lights to underside of cabinets over work area, as close to front of cabinet as possible, screened to keep light out of eyes. (Incandescent is preferable: watch out for glare and flicker from fluorescents.)

Lights attached to the underside of cabinets should be positioned so that no light shines directly into the eyes.

If that isn't possible, use gooseneck lamp (experiment with up to 200 watt bulb, but watch for glare and heat). Place lower edge of lamp shade below eye level.

Mixing ingredients.

SOME SUGGESTIONS:

Glue light and dark squares of plastic sheet to counter in work area: work with dark ingredients on light colored plastic sheets, light ingredients on dark.

Similarly, use dark dishes for mixing flour.

If you can't tell how much you're pouring (spices, salt), pour into your hand first, and *feel* when you have a teaspoonful, half a teaspoonful, etc.

Color contrast is an easy way to improve visibility. Light liquids contrast well with a dark piece of paper glued to the wall; dark liquids show up against the light wall.

How can I tell what cans contain?

Label items at the store where you buy them, while someone is there to help you.

As soon as cans come into the house, get someone (neighbor, delivery man, friend) to identify them. Then mark them — felt stick-ons, plastic labels with different number of dots, varying numbers of rubber bands (simplest).

1

2

PHOTO: COURTESY "AIDS AND APPLIANCES REVIEW,"
THE CARROLL CENTER FOR THE BLIND

PHOTO: COURTESY "AIDS AND APPLIANCES REVIEW,"
THE CARROLL CENTER FOR THE BLIND

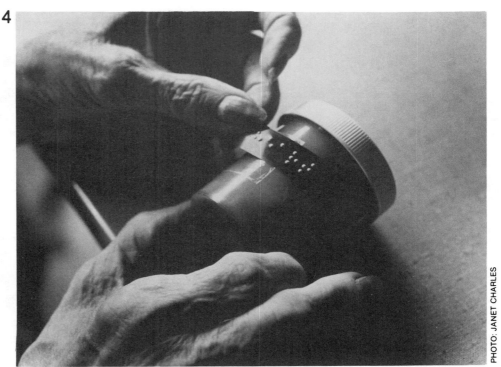

There are all manner of ways to label items; the trick is to use a method that suits you. 1. A simple way is to put rubber bands around cans. 2. Attach Loebel that is the same shape as food in can (in this case an ear of corn). 3. Use large letters. 4. If you read braille, it makes excellent labels.

How can I slice vegetables and prepare food?

SOME SUGGESTIONS:

Use spiked cutting board.

Get Magna Wonder Knife (or similar product) from local hardware store or American Foundation for the Blind: this knife has an adjustable slicing guide that makes it easy and safe to cut slices of a predetermined thickness.

Use cutting board of color that contrasts with food so you can see it better.

Magna Wonder knife has an adjustable guide to allow you to control the thickness of slices, even if you do not see well.

White cutting board provides high contrast that makes it easier to see dark foods you are preparing.

PHOTO: JANET CHARLES

How can I take water from sink to stove/work area without spilling?

SOME SUGGESTIONS:

Put pot in broiler pan, cake pan, tray or cookie sheet with rim and then carry to work area.

Ice cube tray can be filled and carried to freezer using the method described above.

Use larger container such as plastic pitcher or kettle; carry that to stove/work area and fill other container there. (Do not fill to top.)

If your kitchen is large, put pot on cart and wheel it across floor.

Fill pot when it is on stove and do not fill it to the top.

Use suction cup to stabilize dishes on counter or table.

To help you judge liquid level in pots use dark pot (such as Teflon) for light colored liquids, and light-colored pot for dark liquids.

Use a light-colored pot to provide contrast with dark liquids. Note how the wooden spoon stands out against white plate, which in turn contrasts with dark stove. Contrasting tape wrapped around the pot handle helps to make it more visible.

Finding foods in freezer/ refrigerator.

SOME SUGGESTIONS:

Most people have storage systems for placing and locating items in the refrigerator. Putting things in alphabetical order works well. Try to develop a similar system for the freezer; if you can't remember where things are, draw a chart and tape to freezer door. Loebels work very well in the freezer. You can close freezer bags with colored ties to help with identification.

Setting refrigerator/ freezer temperature.

SOME SUGGESTIONS:

Learn to listen for clicks.

Use battery lighted magnifier to read dial.

Mark the dial with raised dots of glue, nail polish, Hi-Marks.

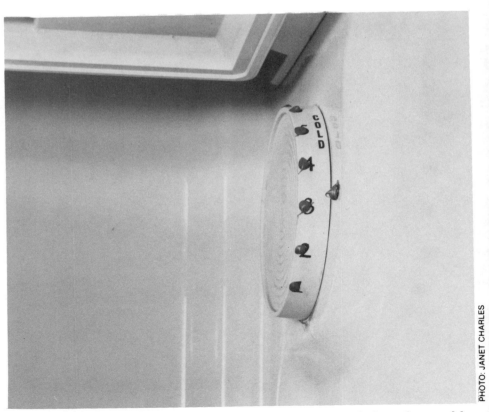

PHOTO: JANET CHARLES

If you can't see well enough to read dials, raised dots formed by glue, nail polish, or Hi Marks (shown here), allow you to feel refrigerator settings by touch.

Finding canned goods in cupboard.

SOME SUGGESTIONS:

Organize your shelves systematically, and label both the shelves and cans. For example, label one shelf fruit, and arrange cans of fruit in alphabetical order. Follow this procedure for vegetables, meats.

Cans may be labelled with large print, different color plastic labels, emobossed or braille tags, Loebels, or devise your own system. (See also p. 32-33.)

Put shelves on the back of cabinet doors (hardware stores often have these easily installed items).

Use lazy susans.

You might find it easier to see and reach for items stored in cabinets below the counter.

Finding utensils in cabinets.

SOME SUGGESTIONS:

Hang most-used pots and utensils from wooden strip and/or peg-board on wall or cabinet.

Organize drawers; plan with friend or make it a family project.

Avoiding hitting head on cupboard doors.

SOME SUGGESTIONS:

Make a habit of closing cupboard doors as soon as you remove or replace an item.

If possible, replace doors with sliding doors.

Paint cupboards brighter colors, so door will stand out against background, or line with bright contact paper.

Knowing when electric fryer/griddle/cooker goes off.

A SUGGESTION:

Even if you can't see the pilot light go off, in most fry pans, etc., you can feel the vibration when current is on.

What kind of stove should I get?

SOME SUGGESTIONS:

The best advice is to get the kind of stove you are used to. It is true that an electric stove does not have to be lit and there is no danger of gas leakage. But an electric stove has the disadvantage of staying hot after you have switched it off, whereas gas burners go off at once and quickly cool. Electric stoves with pushbutton controls have the advantage of not needing to be marked, though you may want to mark the most-used temperature settings with lipstick. Models with buttons near the front are good.

How can I tell when food in the oven is done?

SOME SUGGESTIONS:

Use battery lighted magnifier to examine food.

Test top for doneness with back of spoon, flat part of knife, fork.

Get timer with alarm signal.

Use meat thermometer with raised marks you can feel.

Smell it; taste it.

This meat thermometer can be read by touch. The glass cover has been removed and tactile markings made around the circumference. By feeling the positions of the needle in relation to the raised marks, this woman can tell if the inside of the roast has reached the required temperature.

Reaching electric outlets.

SOME SUGGESTIONS:

Tape, tack, or screw a short extension outlet to wall/cabinet at convenient height; tack wire to wall so it is out of the way.

Using knobs/dials on oven/ stove/ appliances.

SOME SUGGESTIONS:

Put additional lighting over or near appliances.

Use battery lighted magnifier, but be careful not to get hair near burners. It is better to use touch than get too close.

Learn to listen for (or feel) clicks for various settings.

Check if your appliance is from one of many companies (Amana, Sears, Caloric, G.E., Tappan and others) which supply brailled overlays; even if you don't know braille, raised dots can help to identify settings tactually.

Check if company will supply new/larger dials/knobs (easier to feel, easier to read).

Mark dials/knobs yourself: at key points make dots from glue, Hi-Marks, nail polish or drill small holes and insert pegs so you can feel settings.

COOK & KEEP WARM CONTROL

PHOTO: JANET CHARLES

Dots of glue on these stove controls allow you to set temperatures by touch. You need mark only the most-used settings, and move control from these settings to raise or lower the oven temperature.

How can I avoid burning myself?

SOME SUGGESTIONS:

Certain safety precautions should be habitually observed when using the stove. For example:

Develop the habit of turning off oven and stove top dials *before* removing food.

Use a mitt with grip surfaces.

If your gas stove has no pilot light, use long matches, or flint or battery operated lighter.

Remember-ing to turn off stove/ other appli-ances.

Always use a timer. (This habit is essential.)

Timers are important not only for telling how long food has been cooking, but also as reminders to turn off the stove. This yellow timer has ¾" numbers that are easy to see.

For electric appliance use a cut-off timer, with tactual markings, on extension cord hooked into appliance circuit. (Make sure the timer is of high enough wattage.)

As a signal that oven or burner is being used, turn on an additional light as a reminder, and don't turn it off until you turn off the stove.

Check position of knobs.

Hold hand about a foot from stove burner to check for warmth.

A few simple precautions enable you to continue to use your stove safely. For instance, if you are not sure whether the stove is cool, hold your hand 12″ from the burners and feel for warmth.

How can I see what I'm eating?

Additional lighting, preferably from above with dimmer switch, to augment as needed.

Remember where you placed food.

Learn to locate food with cutlery.

Use a pusher.

Take advantage of color contrasts: if food is dark (such as meat), use light dishes on a dark tablecloth or place mat; if light food (fish, cheese, eggs) use dark plates on a white tablecloth.

Do not use clear glass cups or dishes (they become invisible against any surface).

In the Bedroom

In the bedroom, the most important concern should be accident prevention. Along with the bathroom and circulation routes (including the hallway), the bedroom has one of the highest accident rates in the house. This is even more so when you have impaired vision: your eyes adjust slowly to darkness, and are dazzled when the lights go on. You may also frequently have to get up at night; you may forget to put eyeglasses on, or have impaired sense of balance or stiff joints from arthritis.

I can't see for a few minutes after I turn the lights on.

SOME SUGGESTIONS:

Replace wall switch with dimmer switch, and use an extension cord with dimmer switch for bedside lamp.

Keep night light on all night. (Have one in bedroom and bathroom, and along the way if needed.)

Learn to wait until your eyes adjust.

How can I see to put the bedside lamp on?

SOME SUGGESTIONS:

Tape or tack to the headboard an on/off pushbutton switch on an extension cord.

Position small lamp just inside doorway, where it can be switched on easily to help you find bed lamp.

Avoiding electric wire.

SOME SUGGESTIONS:

Get automatic windup reel to take up slack in wires.

Run wires along walls and tape/tack them to walls or baseboard.

Anchor lamps so they won't be pulled over.

Reaching electric outlets.

A SUGGESTION:

Run extension outlet from a regular outlet and tape/tack at a convenient height.

Keeping from falling off my slippers.

Wear good slippers with backs, but only when getting ready for bed and getting up. Rest of time wear shoes.

Don't wear socks alone: they can be even more slippery.

Wear Scandinavian leather-soled ski socks.

How can I avoid running into open doors?

SOME SUGGESTIONS:

Attach door holder to wall, to keep open door firmly in place.

Make a habit of closing door after using closet.

If no need for privacy or warmth, consider taking bedroom door off altogether; you may be able to rehinge it on other side, or convert to sliding door.

Consider using a curtain instead of a door.

How can I keep from bumping into furniture?

SOME SUGGESTIONS:

Put as much furniture as is practically (and esthetically) possible along walls.

No chairs in middle of floor except as needed for possible support/balance.

Try to remove footboard of bed (very lethal in falls); if that isn't possible, learn to make up bed so that thick quilt is over sharp corners of footboard. (For some people, however, the footboard can be useful as a guide or as a support for covers to reduce pressure on feet.)

46

Reaching things on top shelf of closet.

If seeing what you're reaching for is a problem, try to store items in drawers instead.

Use reacher to bring things closer for identification. (A reacher resembles a long scissor with rubber tips for gripping objects.)

Finding things in closet.

Install automatic or pullchain wall light inside closet. Best place is above door, but if shelf blocks out light, install on wall, taking care that it causes minimal glare.

Work out system so that every item has its own place, and put it away in that place as soon as you take it off. It is important that you—not a relative, friend or social worker—work out your own system.

Learn to hang "go-togethers" on same or adjacent hanger so you won't have to hunt next time (man's trousers and jacket and ties; woman's dress, belt, accessories.)

Finding clothes in drawers.

The trick is to organize your clothing so there is a place for everything; always put clothes back in the correct place.

Put dividers in drawers to separate items, so you know where they belong.

If you can see well enough to read it, scotch tape chart on top of dresser if forgetting is problem.

Tie different colored ribbons on drawer pulls as a color-identification system; or paste plastic tape on (with varying numbers of dots) for tactile identification.

Room is always too dark.

SOME SUGGESTIONS:

If necessary change curtains/drapes to let more daylight in.

Consider replacing incandescent lighting with fluorescent; you can now obtain fluorescent bulbs that screw into incandescent fixtures.

Check whether increasing wattage of bulbs is effective. (Try to increase enough so that light is adequate, even when shaded to prevent glare.)

If possible, paint walls light color.

Fluorescent bulbs that screw into regular lamp sockets give far more light than incandescent bulbs — and use less electricity.

PHOTO: JANET CHARLES

Remembering to turn off electric heater.

Use heater with automatic cut-off switch.

Connect up a cut-off timer with tactual markings (available from the American Foundation for the Blind and other sources). Take care not to exceed power capacity of timer.

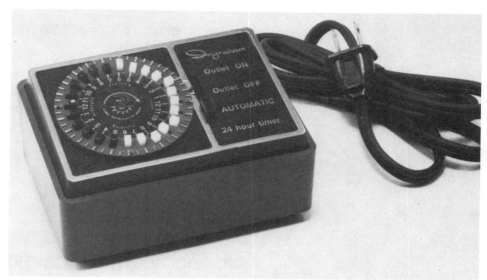

This timer can be set by touch as it had raised dots at 6 A.M., 12 noon, 6 P.M. and midnight. It can turn off appliances (not air conditioners) and lights at hourly intervals.

Avoiding tripping on doorsill/ shoes.

SOME SUGGESTIONS:

If possible, remove sill; if not, plane down to ¼ inch, paint brighter color.

Bevel edges of sill.

Always put shoes and slippers away, in closet or under bed, as soon as you take them off.

Locating small objects on bedside table.

SOME SUGGESTIONS:

Place a gooseneck lamp or adjustable high intensity lamp on table.

Attach bed caddy to side of bed, for smaller objects, tissues, eyeglasses.

Try to put all items in same places every night.

Keep items in box or tray, which will also prevent their falling off the table.

In the Bathroom

The bathroom always requires caution. For older people with impaired vision, the combination of slipperiness, hardness — porcelain fixtures, tile walls, and floor — and glare from highly reflective surfaces can be dangerous. An obvious solution is to replace all switches with dimmer switches.

Keeping from slipping on wet floor.

SOME SUGGESTIONS:

Take care not to spill — especially soapy liquid.

Use floor mat with non-skid backing.

Install wall-to-wall carpeting (quick-dry type) or indoor-outdoor carpeting.

Attach strips of colorful friction-tape to floor.

How can I keep from slipping in tub/shower?

SOME SUGGESTIONS:

Use floor mat with non-skid backing, textured surface.

Attach friction tape or patterned appliques to bottom of tub or shower, to provide non-skid surface.

Install grab bar, towel bar or tub/shower seat.

PHOTO: JANET CHARLES

While this non-skid mat has been placed in the tub to prevent slipping, note how its contrasting color also makes the tub much easier to see. The tub's visibility can also be increased by putting contrasting-colored tape along the edge or draping a contrasting-colored bath mat over it.

Seeing side of tub.

SOME SUGGESTIONS

Drape contrasting bath-mat over tub.

Put broad band of contrasting colored tape on edge of tub.

How can I keep from falling getting in and out of the tub/shower?

SOME SUGGESTIONS:

Put broad band of contrasting colored tape on shower lip.

Put contrasting wall-to-wall floor mat in shower, with non-skid backing and textured surface (also helps you find dropped soap).

Fix grab bar (or additional towel bar) in strategic location(s).

Move slowly and carefully.

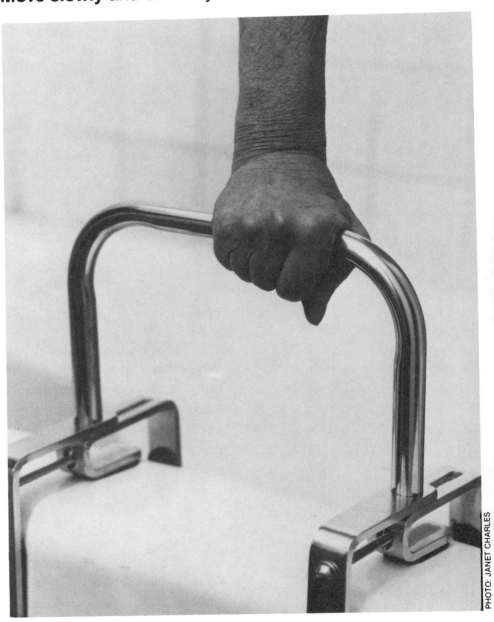

PHOTO: JANET CHARLES

Grab bar easily attached to tub helps prevent slipping as you get into and out of it.

How can I see how much water is in tub?

SOME SUGGESTIONS:

Float a brightly colored toy in water.

Feel with hand, but take care water is not too hot.

Put contrasting stripe at usual level of water and fill to that point.

Put additional lighting over tub/shower, but fixture must be impervious to damp.

How can I avoid scalding myself?

SOME SUGGESTIONS:

Learn how far to rotate faucet(s) for correct temperature.

Use hand-held shower, so water can be tested on hand.

Turn on cold water first, then add the hot; when turning off, turn off hot first, then cold.

Finding towels/ washrag.

SOME SUGGESTIONS:

Switch to colors that contrast with color (or gray value) of place where it will hang.

Always hang up in same place when not using.

Finding soap.

SOME SUGGESTIONS:

Switch to liquid soap dispenser, wall mounted or free-standing.

Use brightly colored soap.

Place soap in same place every day.

Use soap on a rope and hang it around neck, or from shower.

How can I find out what I weigh?

Use a scale that has waist-high dial.

Put bright adhesive tape at usual weight; any difference from this is readily detected.

Use scale with movable weights; you can feel clicks as weights are moved and can feel when moving arm is balanced.

Brushing teeth.

SOME SUGGESTIONS:

Switch to dark toothbrush (against light background).

Squeeze toothpaste into palm or finger and wipe it up from there.

Squeeze paste onto finger and then put paste on teeth.

How can I tell my medicines apart?

SOME SUGGESTIONS:

Organize medicine cabinets so important items are always in the same place.

Keep medicines in alphabetical order.

If you cannot identify medications by size/shape/color of bottle or package, use adhesive tape (one/two/three strips, vertical/horizontal/diagonal) or varying number of rubber bands.

Label pill bottles with individual plastic alphabet letters, e.g., N for nitroglycerin, V for valium.

Separate medications and keep where appropriate: breakfast pills in kitchen, nighttime pills in bedroom.

How can I avoid hitting my head on door of medicine cabinet?

SOME SUGGESTIONS:

Change to sliding door.

Cover corner or edge with bright tape, or with soft padding.

Make a habit of always closing cabinet doors.

Can't see to give myself injections.

SOME SUGGESTIONS:

Check with your doctor or nurse as to what will work best for you.

Use syringe magnifier or use battery lit hand-held magnifier, or stand magnifier.

Use pre-set syringe: doctor or nurse will have to set the syringe for correct dosage. Premeasured dosages may be available.

Use tactile syringes.

Use insul-gages if measuring insulin.

Combing my hair, putting on make-up.

SOME SUGGESTIONS:

Use a wall-mounted mirror with an extension arm; a magnifying mirror could help.

Use neck-held mirror.

Use illuminated mirror.

Seeing toilet seat/toilet tissue.

SOME SUGGESTIONS:

Replace with dark/contrasting colored seat.

Use color contrasting tissue.

Use a frame with arm like a chair which fits over toilet seat and can be grasped easily.

In the Living Room

I'm afraid of falling.

A SUGGESTION:

You may feel safer if you have hand contact with some object every few feet — for guidance, for balance, and for recovery if you stumble. Rather than having wide open spaces, as in the typical living room, place furniture alongside traffic routes, so you can move from one to another — high-backed chairs are good.

Keeping from hurting yourself on the furniture.

SOME SUGGESTIONS:

If possible, remove tables (everything that juts out or has a horizontal projection is a menace), and most especially low coffee tables.

Drape tables with cloth.

How can I avoid slipping and stumbling?

SOME SUGGESTIONS:

Remove/replace/change around worn carpeting.

Tack down or use double sided tape on all runners/area rugs.

Tape down all edges in line of traffic.

Do not wax or polish wood floors. If possible, cover with non-skid rug, carpeting or textured runners.

Use non-skid wax with minimal buffing.

I can't see what I'm doing in there.

SOME SUGGESTIONS:

This can be a result of the subdued "mood" lighting that is popular in living rooms. Use more powerful ceiling lighting and install dimmer switches, to allow subdued effect when desired. Also add floor lamps for occasions when even more illumination is needed.

Check if daytime problem is caused by drapes, curtains, shades, venetian blinds over windows.

Use light/bright color on walls, drapes, couch(es) and chairs.

On Steps/Stairs

Most older people prefer to stay in the homes in which they have been living all along. But if there is one compelling reason (aside from size) for moving, it can be summed up in one word: steps. Not only because of the energy needed to climb and descend but also because steps can be perilous. For visually impaired older people they become especially dangerous, as it is difficult for them to know where a staircase begins and ends. Most falls occur on the top step coming down from the landing, where visual control over the first step is important. To make steps safer, all adaption components should be considered and perhaps all used.

Making steps safer.

SOME SUGGESTIONS:

Top and bottom should be well-lighted, accenting first step and tread.

Non-glare localized lighting on each step helps (as in darkened theaters).

Mark the leading edge of each step, on both the runner (tread) and the riser, with a paint or non-skid material that has a color and grey value high in contrast with the color and grey value of the stairs themselves. 3M reflecting tape can be effective for this purpose. These markings should run the entire width of the step, and be two or three inches wide on both the runner and the riser. A wider marking can be used to highlight the top step itself.

It is helpful if material on leading edge is textured. Learn to grip bannister (handrail) and *feel* for steps with foot.

PHOTO: JANET CHARLES

Contrasting tape on these stairs turns a vague blur into well-defined areas of light and dark indicating position of steps.

Reaching the handrail.

Paint handrail in a light/bright contrasting color. It should extend past the top and bottom steps for easy grasping.

Identifying the end of the steps.

A SUGGESTION:

A contrasting color should be used on landings (top and bottom).

In the Hallway

How can I see where I'm going?

SOME SUGGESTIONS:

Use additional ceiling or wall-mounted fluorescent or incandescent lighting. If hallway is long, use track-lighting (if not too expensive).

Install hallway runner, dark in center, light colored near walls, to serve as guide.

Put a rail guide along hall.

Textured wallpaper can provide tactile cues.

How can I know where the sill is?

SOME SUGGESTIONS:

Remove sill, or plane it down to ¼ inch and paint it brightly.

How can I avoid slipping and stumbling?

SOME SUGGESTIONS:

Remove or replace worn runner.

Use high friction runner instead of polished floor.

Can't see light switch.

SOME SUGGESTIONS:

Use luminescent light switch plate or switch with night light outlet.

Put color contrasting tape around switch.

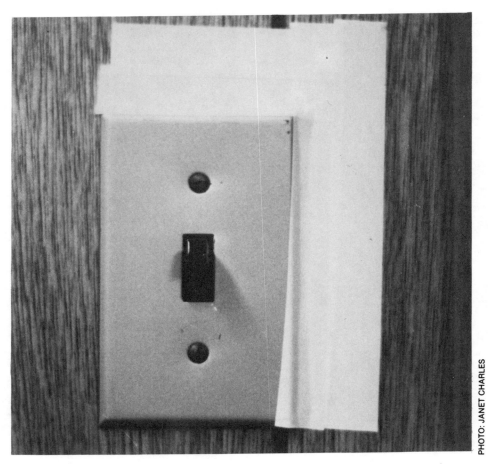

Contrasting tape around the light switch makes it stand out against the wall.

PHOTO: JANET CHARLES

Handling Work and Recreation

Reading tape measure.

SOME SUGGESTIONS:

Use magnifier.

Use adapted tape measure that has holes to indicate inch and half-inch intervals.

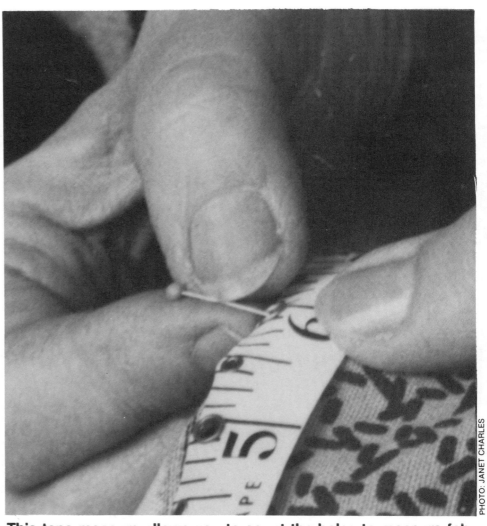

This tape measure allows you to count the holes to measure fabrics. Note that the large heads on the pins make them easier to see.

Knitting/ crocheting.

SOME SUGGESTIONS:

Use brightly-colored needles for contrast.

Use chest-held magnifier, which leaves both hands free.

Seeing to read, do close work and write.

SOME SUGGESTIONS:

Use task-oriented incandescent lighting, to supplement general room lighting. To avoid glare, the light source should be positioned above and behind you.

During day, light from window can be good for reading.

Take advantage of natural light whenever possible: Light from this window evenly illuminates the page this man is reading.

If work surface produces glare, change for matte/dull top. If you must use existing surface, there are artists' spray fixatives which will kill reflections and glare.

When writing, if edges of paper seem to disappear, place paper on dark surface.

Use lined paper.

Write with felt tip pen, which will give broad, legible strokes.

Use writing guide, available from AFB and other sources.

For writing checks, you can get a custom-made template from AFB.

Broad strokes from a felt tip pen are very readable. A lens mounted on a goose-neck lamp enables this woman to read the small type in the 'phone book.

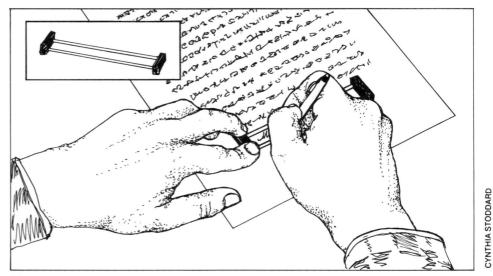

Signature guide defines the area in which you can sign when you can't see too well.

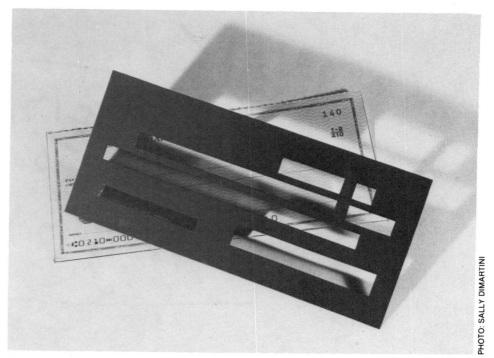

Custom-made template matches your own checks and guides your hand to the lines you fill out.

Dialing a number on the phone.

SOME SUGGESTIONS:

Attach a large and raised number template—available for both dial and push-button phones from AFB. (See p. 66–67 for various phone adaptations.)

On pushbutton phones learn positions of numbers—left column reads 1, 4, 7; middle runs 2, 5, 8, 0; right column is 3, 6, 9.

Check out (free) operator assisted service for elderly and disabled people in your community, as well as any special telephone equipment available for visually impaired persons (some are free).

For emergencies you can dial 911—the numbers are easy to locate on either dial or pushbutton phones.

Learn which holes represent which number (and letter) then dial by placing first four fingers in first four holes—little finger in the "one," ring finger in the "two," middle finger in the "three," and index finger in "four." Move index finger to dial 5, 6, 7, 8, 9, 0.

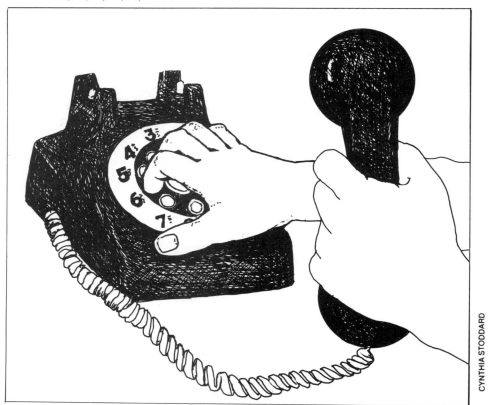

Positioning your fingers as shown makes it easy to find numbers on the dial, the index finger moving to other numbers as required.

These easy-to-read numbers have adhesive backing and are easily attached to regular 'phone buttons.

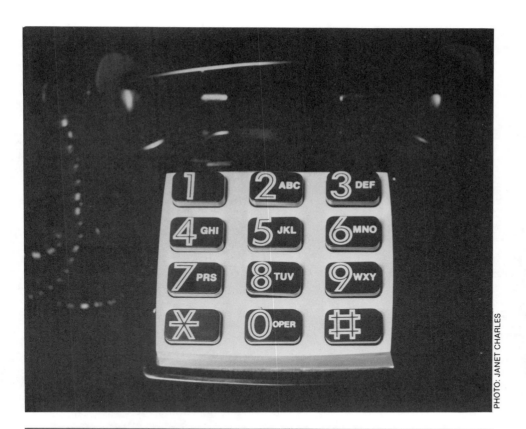

The large buttons fit over regular buttons (upper). Touch dialing is easier if you remember the numbers in each column. Big Button 'phone (lower), available from your Phone Store, has 2″ square buttons that make dialing easy.

Threading a needle.

Use **metal-loop** needle threader or self-threading needles.

For **heavier** work, you can use spread-eye needles.

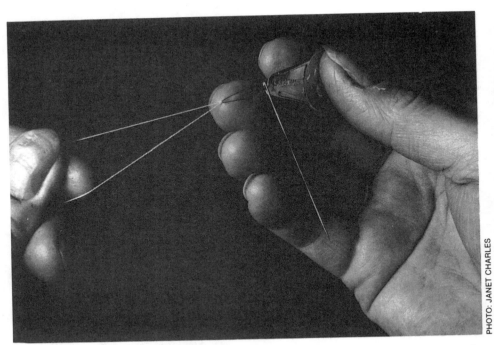

PHOTO: JANET CHARLES

It's easy to thread a needle with this simple little device. You push the metal loop through the eye of the needle, put the thread through the loop, and then pull both loop and thread back through the eye.

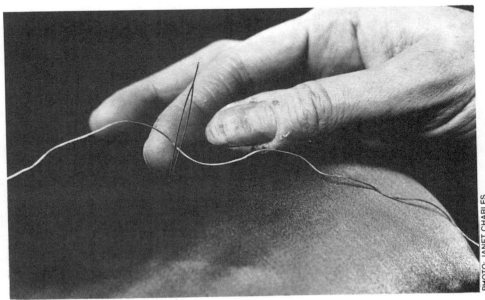

PHOTO: JANET CHARLES

This spread eye needle is split along its length, forming a large eye that is easy to thread. It is best for rather coarse thread.

Working the washing machine.

SOME SUGGESTIONS:

Use task-lighting, but watch for glare from porcelain surface.

If you cannot see dial settings, listen for clicks or try to feel settings.

Use hand magnifier, battery lighted magnifier.

Mark key settings with crayon, lipstick, colored tape, or felt tip pen.

Tooth picks or beads glued on with epoxy glue work well.

Check with manufacturer or dealer to find out whether they will supply braille or large letter dials or overlays.

Ironing.

SOME SUGGESTIONS:

Run hand over ironed part to determine if wrinkles have been removed.

Mark key settings on iron with tape or felt tip pen.

Use raised ironing board, if position is not too tiring for your arm.

Sit down while ironing.

Install hook in ceiling or wall to keep ironing cord out of the way.

Use solid colored, not patterned, ironing board cover.

Finding articles dropped on floor.

SOME SUGGESTIONS:

Squat rather than bend down and move hands systematically over floor surface.

If you have difficulty squatting or bending, use a broom with a wide head to check a large area for the presence of an object.

Playing cards and other games.

SOME SUGGESTIONS:

Many large size, large print, games and cards are available. Some games have braille markings. All these games are designed to be played by people with good vision as well as by those who do not see well.

A wide variety of games have been adapted by AFB and others to allow blind and visually impaired people to continue to play. All the adapted games can also be played by those with good vision. These cards have extra large numbers that can be read by those with poor vision, and also have braille dots for those who cannot see the print.

The raised ridges around the squares of this Othello board keep discs from sliding. Discs are marked for tactual identification.

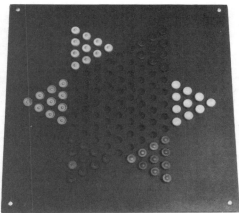

The pegs of this adapted Chinese checkers game are in the usual range of colors, but their tops have been given different shapes so the players who do not see well can feel which are their pegs.

Watching television.

SOME SUGGESTIONS:

Many older people stop looking at the TV and just listen as though it were a radio. (You can buy radios that receive TV audio only.)

Some who do watch, prefer a small screen because when they sit close they can see all of the screen. Others prefer a large TV, which can still be seen when they sit back from the screen. You should determine for yourself whether you can see color or black and white better.

A light should also be on in the room—a floor lamp or other light positioned where it does not reflect in screen or cause glare.

(For additional suggestions and tips, see *Prescriptions for Independence,* available from the American Foundation for the Blind, or call your local agency for the blind and visually impaired.)

Reading rulers, instruments, scales.

SOME SUGGESTIONS:

Use magnifier.

Use adapted tools such as raised line rules, electronic levels, scales with raised dots.

Make your your own templates that are the exact length of measurements you often take.

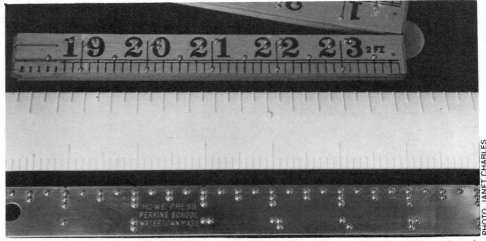

Examples of adapted rulers: With braille numbers (top); with raised lines (center); and raised dots with braille numbers (bottom).

PHOTO: JANET CHARLES

How can I continue to use my workshop?

SOME SUGGESTIONS:

Good lighting is essential. Combine good overhead lighting with an adjustable swing arm lamp that can be moved in closely for tasks requiring fine control of hand movements.

Organize both your tools and work area. You can mount graduated tools such as screwdriver sets or wrenches in sequence by size.

Label size of tools by large print numbers, raised dots, or by whatever labeling system works best for you.

Use reflective or color-contrasting tape, or luminous paint to make tools contrast with work area.

Use magnifiers. Chest held magnifiers or magnifiers mounted on flexible "gooseneck" stands allow you to use both hands.

Safety goggles/glasses can be obtained with prescription lenses.

PHOTO: SUSAN ISLAM

PHOTO: JANET CHARLES

Contrasting tape around tool handles makes them easier to see. Notice how this man has placed his tools on a dark background to provide good contrast.

Just Outside the Door

The focus of this Handbook has been *inside* the home, and on adaptations there. For most visually impaired older people, the world does not come to a stop at the front door: a few words about some aspects of that "home range," shrunken though it may be, are germane here. The following problems are likely to be encountered by people who live in rental housing or in high-rise apartment buildings.

Getting off the elevator at the right floor.

SOME SUGGESTIONS:

When the elevator door opens you may not be quite sure where you are. There may be a number on the landing door, but what if it's faded or you can't make it out? It can be so simple: put a small dab of glue—at a place convenient for you—on the elevator side of the landing door; and perhaps two dabs on the door at the lobby floor. One touch tells you which floor you are on.

You can ask the building management to make your floor easier to identify.

Making sure you're at your own apartment.

A few rubber bands around the door knob will serve to identify it.

Paste a decal or contrasting color felt cut-out on your own apartment door.

Locating your mail box.

Stick a dab of glue, a piece of colored tape, or some easily identified object on it.

Count how far your mail box is from the end of the row of boxes.

Identifying keys.

If feasible, keep keys in order.

Use colored keys, which are now available.

Use keys with different shaped heads.

A Little Further from the Door

Go just a little further beyond the door, to two important facilities in the lives of older people, men and women alike: supermarkets and laundromats. These places serve not only their commercial purposes, but also a social purpose — as popular meeting points for many older people in the community.

Supermarkets: When the world starts shrinking as a result of visual impairments, the supermarket often becomes less appealing than the mom-and-pop stores, which provide personal service (though perhaps at higher prices).

For people with impaired vision the chief problem is supermarket lighting— too little *and* too much of it. Too *little* to find, let alone read, the small print on the items desired. And too *much* light—in the form of glare — from the front windows. Dr. Leon Pastalan has produced slides showing what the visually impaired person sees from the back of the market looking toward the front windows: noth-

Finding items in the supermarket can be difficult when you don't see well. Furthermore, most supermarkets are badly lit, with on the one hand aisles that are too dim, and on the other hand excessive glare streaming through the windows. One helpful tip is to learn to find products by the patterns of light and dark they form on the shelves. Here, the light area indicates where the mayonnaise is, while the darker area beyond shows the presence of ketchup. Once you have identified the general pattern, then a magnifier may help you to pick out your favorite brand or flavor.

ing but darkness and a bright blur. Mylar shades, venetian blinds and plastic sheeting all cut down on the glare, but at the expense of too much lost light.

Perhaps those supermarkets located in retirement communities and areas with large numbers of senior citizens will—for economic reasons—be the first to implement the knowledge already gained about the benefits of polarized plate glass, spot lighting, enhanced lighting, and more readable packaging. Such adaptations may catch on when stores find that younger customers like the changes too.

Laundromats: In a Department of Housing and Urban Development study in 1977, older visually impaired people complained that they couldn't see the dial and selector settings on either washers or dryers. Apartment dwellers may be able to ask for help. But, as an example of what community agencies for the visually impaired can do, Vernon Metcalf (Miami Lighthouse) reports that owners of laundromats in his area have no objection to his agency's people coming in and pasting dots on all machines, according to a code which all of his clients understand.

Community agencies: Many visually impaired older people might be induced to leave their homes more often if community groups paid more attention to their visual difficulties. Community agencies for visually impaired persons could perform a useful service by looking at churches, synagogues, and senior centers, where older people gather together, and offering suggestions for making these facilites more convenient for older people. Sometimes even the local senior center, which should be highly conscious of the changes which aging brings, is unaware of the problems it poses for the visually impaired person who comes in.

Perhaps the most negative component is lighting: the complex interaction between lighting levels, sources, and glare has created an abominable visual environment, even in some of the best institutions. Among the lighting problems are flickering fluorescent lights, "mood" (subdued) lighting, exposed bulbs and the typical "downlighting" of lobbies and other large areas.

In certain buildings presumably designed for older people, some designers have experimented with bold and trendy interiors, such as bright colors, supergraphics, or even full-scale decorative objects from other environments: awnings, fountains, and crystal. The result is contrived and jarring. A safe, functional building should have precedence over the visual effect of the usual nonfunctional design.

Some helpful adaptations may not be cost-effective, e.g., synthetic speech that announces floor numbers and directions on elevators. Still, elevator buttons can be identified by large/raised markings at relatively little cost. There can be well-lit large number indicators on the landings; landing areas in front of the elevator can be distinctively painted or marked.

As for stairways, the suggestions for enhanced safety in the home environment apply with far greater force and validity in public/community settings. And what was said about hallways is even more relevant to corridors — with certain additions: Corridors become booby-traps if there are wall-hung ashtrays, water fountains, telephones, all of which can't be seen because of glare from the window at the end of the corridor. Glass doors become dangerous obstacles to a person who can't see well. Brightly colored tape may be all that is needed to make glass doors visible.

Information doesn't inform if the person it is intended for can't even tell it's there, let alone read it — if it is too small, doesn't have color contrast, is too high up or too far away. Restrooms, which could easily be marked with large/raised letters and color contrasted graphics, are not readily accessible if you need someone's help to determine where the graphics are and what they say.

If such problems exist even in a senior center, a little consciousness-raising on the part of the community agency for blind and visually impaired people is called for. In fact, that agency, by pointing to its own environmental adaptations, can serve as a model for other community facilities and agencies, a demonstration that effective modifications can be made with minimal effort and cost, but with maximum benefit to users and potential users. Older people with visual impairments could help to choose adaptations and test them, as a double check on their validity.

If more facilities are adapted to the needs of visually impaired older people, and if more of them are attracted to these facilities, then perhaps the world of older people might stop shrinking. And even begin to expand again.

To Enhance the Quality of Life

Given the great number of elderly people with impaired vision living at home, why has so little been done in the way of environmental modifications and adaptation? It may be because one of the abiding myths of our times is that as people grow old they shrink, sometimes physically but always mentally. They are expected to withdraw from the world, perhaps to become "senile."

We tend to think of old age as the end, not the beginning of a new phase of life. Even in the field of blindness and visual impairment the emphasis has been on technology and adaptive devices for education, for work, for active recreation—but not for the home. The homes of many older persons therefore provide an abominable visual environment that makes their disability worse—an environment in which poor sight, poor lighting, the presence of avoidable obstacles, and lack of help all combine to make life unlivable.

Nevertheless, evidence abounds, that the home does not have to be an enemy. Technology already exists to provide a protective—or even prosthetic—environment for visually impaired older people. There are remote control systems that automatically turn appliances, lights and alarms on and off — and that even tell a person when it is time to take medication. An architect and a designer can "tune" a room or a house to individual requirements, making it mellower or more brilliant or warmer, by changing size, shape, proportions, colors, or furnishings. Windows can be made of polarized glass to keep out daylight glare; dimmer switches, task-oriented lighting, focused hall and stairway lighting (or no steps at all) can make it easier to use limited vision; and tactile cues can provide guidance as well as mental stimulation. Clocks and appliances programmed to announce themselves and their functions in synthetic speech can be installed. The snag is that much of this is for tomorrow's homes, and people with visual problems now cannot wait; for them help delayed is help denied.

Fortunately, there is no need to wait. Many of the simpler adaptations described in this book can be done easily, cheaply, and *now*. To make any home more livable for the visually impaired older person— your mother, your father, your aunt, a client, or yourself — there will never be a better day to begin than today.

Appendix
Dr. Leon Pastalan's Empathic Model

No architect would continue to design imposing building entrances at the top of a long flight of steps if he himself had to use the building everyday — in a wheelchair. "No architect who had trouble with his own legs would be so inconsiderate," wrote humorist Clarence Day, who suffered from crippling arthritis. "Whenever we citizens engage a new architect to put up a building, let it be stipulated in the contract that the Board of Aldermen shall break his legs first. . . ."

Until quite recently most architects and designers had shown little understanding of the problems of people with limited vision, and little sensitivity to their needs. "Comparatively extensive research has been carried out as far as personal technical aids are concerned," says a study by Sweden's International Commission on Technical Aids Centre, but "surprisingly little has been done to improve the physical environment." As a result we have few examples of environments which truly maximize remaining visual capabilities, or which encourage use of alternative senses.

"There hasn't been a single national